S0-ACV-968

HIP-HOP Hitmakers

THE STORY OF
INTERSCOPE
RECORDS

diane bailey

Mason Crest Publishers
Philadelphia

HIP-HOP
hitmakers

Mason Crest
370 Reed Road
Broomall, PA 19008
www.masoncrest.com

Printed and bound in the United States of America.

CPSIA Compliance Information: Batch #HHH040112-6.
For further information, contact Mason Crest at 1-866-MCP-Book

First printing
1 3 5 7 9 8 6 4 2

Library of Congress Cataloging-in-Publication Data

Bailey, Diane, 1966-
  The story of Interscope Records / by Diane Bailey.
      p. cm. — (Hip-hop hitmakers)
  Includes bibliographical references and index.
  ISBN 978-1-4222-2115-0 (hc)
  ISBN 978-1-4222-2128-0 (pb)
  ISBN 978-1-4222-9467-3 (ebook)
  1. Interscope Records—Juvenile literature. 2. Sound recording industry—United States—
Juvenile literature. I. Title.
  ML3792.I64B35 2012
  338.7'61782421649—dc23
                                           2011035328

Photo credits: © Apple Inc.: 42; Associated Press: 19; Getty Images: cover; Time & Life Pictures / Getty Images: 24; courtesy Interscope Records: 39; Library of Congress: 10; PR Newswire: 27, 30, 50 (top); used under license from Shutterstock, Inc.: 15; Celebrityphoto / Shutterstock.com: 34; Anthony Correia / Shutterstock.com: 8 (bottom); Helga Esteb / Shutterstock.com: 4, 7, 8 (top), 35, 54; Mat Hayward / Shutterstock.com: 18; Adam J. Sablich / Shutterstock.com: 31, 50 (bottom); Joe Seer / Shutterstock.com: 33, 36, 44, 46, 53; TDC Photography / Shutterstock.com: 49; U.S. Senate collection: 23 (bottom); White House photo: 23 (top).

3 1558 00276 9156

Contents

Interscope artist Lady Gaga arrives at a 2010 awards show wearing a dress made from meat. Since the label was founded in 1990, Interscope has introduced many unusual and talented performers.

new kid on the block

The two men weren't much alike. Jimmy Iovine came from a working-class family in Brooklyn, New York. His father was a dockworker. Ted Field was born into a life of privilege. His family, one of the wealthiest and most famous in Chicago, owned the *Chicago Sun-Times* newspaper, *Parade* magazine, and *The World Book Encyclopedia*.

Iovine started his career at the bottom. His first job in the music business was as an assistant at a recording studio. He ran errands and helped set up equipment. Field's road was paved with family money. When he turned 25, he inherited more than $200 million and became co-owner of Field Enterprises, the family's media empire.

Iovine gradually won a reputation for helping musical artists hone their sound. Field started his own Hollywood production company, which produced several hit movies.

Their worlds seemed completely different. But Jimmy Iovine and Ted Field had one thing in common: a love of music. And after meeting through a mutual friend, Iovine and Field decided to launch their own record company. That *label,* Interscope Records, would become one of the most remarkable success stories in the music industry.

THE PRODUCER

Jimmy Iovine was born in 1953. While growing up during the 1960s, he played in a band with some of his friends. At age 19, he got a job at the Record Plant recording studio in New York City. At first, the work wasn't too glamorous. Iovine did everything from cleaning floors to moving equipment to fetching food and refreshments. But he enjoyed the atmosphere. He loved being around music and musicians.

After putting in some time at the Record Plant, Iovine began moving up through the ranks there. He became a sound engineer, recording and mixing songs for albums. Early on, he got to work with one of his idols—former Beatle John Lennon. He also worked with Bruce Springsteen. Iovine was a sound engineer for *Born to Run,* the 1975 album that launched Springsteen to superstardom.

Two years later, Iovine got his first opportunity as a record producer. In the music industry, producers are very important. Basically, they manage the entire recording process. This includes technical aspects, such as ensuring that the engineer captures the desired sound. But it also includes creative aspects. For example, a producer might decide that a particular song would be more appealing with a faster beat.

Interscope co-founder Jimmy Iovine remains the head of the label.

The producer might call for a stronger bass line. The producer might add horns, strings, or background vocals. In ways such as these, a producer can help shape an artist's or a band's sound. There are many talented musicians. Sometimes the difference between a hit album and an album that sells poorly is a talented producer.

Iovine's first experience as a producer was with a Brooklyn-based band called Flame. The band released two albums but never made it big.

In 1977, Iovine was taking a break at the studio when Patti Smith walked in. A punk rocker, Smith had two previous albums to her credit. Neither had sold well, despite critical acclaim for the first, *Horses* (1975). Iovine and Smith began talking. "With Patti, I saw things in her that she didn't even see," Iovine recalled.

> She wondered why her records didn't sell more, and I told her it was because her first album showed only one side of her—the punk/poet thing. To me, there was a lot more, a sort of mix between the street poet aura of Jim Morrison and the energy and excitement of the Rolling Stones. I thought she needed to put all sides on a record to really reach everyone with her music.

Iovine wasn't shy about telling Smith what he thought. She welcomed the input. In fact, she asked him to produce her next album.

In the 1970s and 1980s, Iovine made a name for himself as a producer of hit albums for rockers like U2 (top) and Bruce Springsteen (right).

The result was *Easter*, which was released in 1978. For the album, Iovine had Smith sing a song she had co-written with Bruce Springsteen called "Because the Night." The song became a successful *single*. The music magazine *Billboard* keeps charts of the most popular albums and songs. "Because the Night" reached number 13 on the Billboard Hot 100 chart and helped drive sales of the album.

A year after the release of *Easter*, Iovine produced an album that helped another artist achieve a commercial breakthrough. This time it was *Damn the Torpedoes* by Tom Petty and the Heartbreakers. The album went *platinum*, meaning it sold a million copies.

Iovine's services as a producer were now in great demand. In addition to Lennon, Springsteen, Smith, and Petty, he produced albums for artists such as U2, the Pretenders, and Stevie Nicks of Fleetwood Mac.

By the late 1980s, Iovine had spent years working in studios. He'd learned that recording was mostly long hours and hard work. "When I first went into the studio with John Lennon and Bruce Springsteen," he recalled years later, "I thought making records was going to be fun, like going to a Rolling Stones concert. But fun had nothing to do with it. Fun wasn't even on the menu."

THE TYCOON

Ted Field, meanwhile, had been learning his own lessons. Field—who, like Jimmy Iovine, was born in 1953—had a rocky start in the business world. After coming into his inheritance, Field clashed with his half brother, Marshall Field V, over how to run the family business. In the early 1980s, Ted Field forced the breakup of the family's media empire. Field Enterprises' TV stations were sold off, as was the *Chicago Sun-Times*.

Ted Field's share from these sales amounted to more than $250 million. He plunged some of his money into his Hollywood production company, started in 1982. His first projects went nowhere, however, and Field lost money. "He was footing the entire bill," noted a Hollywood lawyer named Skip Brittenham. Field eventually recognized the importance of partnering with a studio. This would help his production company finance and *distribute* its movies. Field soon became skilled at making movie deals. During the 1980s, his company produced a number of profitable films.

The Field family's fortune originally came from a successful department store called Marshall Field's. Ted Field's great-great grandfather had started the business in Chicago in 1852.

But Field wasn't satisfied with simply making money. "I wanted to do something that meant something in my life," he recalled.

Music meant something in Field's life. He'd always loved attending concerts and was an avid amateur drummer. Field decided to pick the brain of a friend, Paul McGuinness, about the record business. McGuinness was manager of the band U2. He knew Jimmy Iovine, who had produced two U2 albums. McGuinness introduced Field to the music producer.

A PARTNERSHIP

Iovine and Field hit it off. Field respected Iovine's knack for spotting gifted artists and helping them develop. Iovine recognized that savvy business skills were necessary to succeed in the music industry, and Field had those skills. But Iovine also saw that Field was more than just a businessman, just as Field saw that Iovine was more than just a good producer. "The magic in this dynamic between me and Jimmy," Field later told *Time* magazine, "is that all my life people saw me as a kid who inherited money. Jimmy was one of the first to see that I had creative ability in addition to business ability, and I helped Jimmy because I saw that he had incredible business instincts."

The two men dreamed of bringing new music to the public. They decided to pool their talents.

In 1990, with about $30 million, they launched Interscope Records. Field kicked in $15 million of his own money. Some of the remainder of the start-up money came from Atlantic Records, a larger company. Atlantic also agreed to distribute Interscope's records. This was important. Making a record is a lot easier than selling it. That requires money for advertising. There also needs to be a system for getting the record into stores. Setting all that up from scratch would be extremely expensive. Since Atlantic was already a successful company, it had those systems in place.

FIRST EFFORTS

Interscope's first release was from a Latino rapper named Gerardo. His album was called *Mo' Ritmo*. It reached number 36 on the Billboard 200 albums chart, and number 64 on the R&B/Hip hop charts. Mo' Ritmo's hit single, "Rico Suave," went *gold*. This meant it sold 500,000 copies.

Next up for the label was an album from the hip-hop group Marky Mark and the Funky Bunch. The album went gold in 1991, and platinum in 1992.

Neither Gerardo or Marky Mark and the Funky Bunch had long careers as performers. Gerardo has been called a *one-hit wonder*. However, he went on to become an A&R executive at Interscope. A&R (artists and repertoire) executives are in charge of finding new musicians to *sign* to the label.

The fact that neither of Interscope's first two artists turned out to be big stars was hardly a sign of failure. Thousands of artists want to make it in the music business. Very few actually get there.

Interscope also signed the alternative rock band Primus in 1990. The band already had a small group of fans. Now they had a label to help sell their records. Their third album was called *Sailing the Seas of Cheese*. It had several hit singles and went gold.

Interscope was part of Atlantic Records. In turn, Atlantic Records was part of a bigger company called Time Warner. Time Warner had helped Interscope get started. However, Time Warner didn't have any "creative control." Interscope didn't have to receive permission from its parent company about what records to make. The company could record any music it wanted. This freedom also came with risk. Interscope could succeed big—or it could fail big.

THE SCOPE OF INTERSCOPE

Interscope Records was one of several companies that carried the Interscope name. With his inherited fortune, Ted Field founded a film production company called Interscope Communications in 1982. This company made dozens of movies, including *Revenge of the Nerds* (1984), *Three Men and a Baby* (1987), *Bill & Ted's Excellent Adventure* (1989), *Arachnophobia* (1990), *The Hand that Rocks the Cradle* (1992), and *Jumanji* (1995). In 2003, Interscope Communications went out of business. However, Field still works as a film producer through his company Radar Pictures.

Field also liked racing cars. He formed another company called Interscope Racing. It had a team that competed in big racing events such as the Indianapolis 500.

going gangsta

In its first year, Interscope Records enjoyed a couple of modest successes. But it didn't have a strong personality as a company. Interscope executives saw an opportunity in rap music. Rap had become a distinct musical style in the 1970s. In the 1980s, it still was just a small part of the overall music scene. That would start to change in the early 1990s. And Interscope would be a big part of it.

THE ORIGINS OF RAP

In 1979, a group called the Sugarhill Gang recorded the song "Rapper's Delight." It was the first hip-hop song to be a big hit. However, the whole hip-hop lifestyle had started years before. Hip-hop included music, dancing, and graffiti art. It began in New York City, especially in a part of the city called the Bronx. The Bronx was home to many African-American and Latino youths.

At parties, DJs (disc jockeys) would play songs that had strong beats. Performers would talk over the music, often in rhyme. This was called "rapping." Sometimes, rappers would hold contests with each other. The melody was not that important in rap. Instead, it was the beat and rhythm of the song that mattered. The content of the *lyrics* was also important.

Many early rappers lived in poor neighborhoods. Often these neighborhoods suffered from widespread drug abuse and violence. Not surprisingly, drugs and violence became common themes in rap songs.

In the mid-1980s, a specialized kind of rap music developed. "Gangsta rap" was hard-core. It was very violent and very *graphic*. A lot of people—including a lot of rappers—didn't like it.

DEATH ROW RECORDS

One early gangsta rap group was called N.W.A. The group came from Compton, California, a city in the greater Los Angeles area. Compton was known for its street gangs and for its high crime rate. In 1988, N.W.A. released an album called *Straight Outta Compton* on the Ruthless Records label. Ruthless was a small label and did little to promote *Straight Outta Compton*. But the album sold surprisingly well. It helped start the whole gangsta rap movement.

Several members of N.W.A. became unhappy with Ruthless Records and left the label. In 1991, one former member of the group, Dr. Dre, teamed up with another person who had grown up in Compton, Marion "Suge" Knight. The two men wanted to create a record label that specialized in hard-core rap. It would be called Death Row Records.

Dr. Dre was already an experienced producer. He had helped produce a lot of acts when he was with Ruthless Records. Knight had business connections. He was a former football player, celebrity bodyguard, and concert promoter. In 1987, he decided to form a music publishing company. Later he began a company that managed musicians' careers.

DR. DRE

Dr. Dre was named for music. He was born Andre Romelle Young in 1965. His middle name came from his dad's rhythm and blues band, the Romells.

Young wasn't a good student, but he found his passion in music. In the 1980s, he started hanging out at clubs and became a DJ. He adopted the stage name Dr. J, the nickname of basketball superstar Julius Erving. Later Young changed his stage name to Dr. Dre. This was a combination of Dr. J and the second syllable of his first name, Andre. Dre called himself the "master of mixology." That was not because of his name, but because he liked to mix songs together!

In 1984, Dre became a member of the rap group World Class Wreckin' Cru. Two years later, with rapper Ice Cube and four others, he formed N.W.A. That group would become known as one of the pioneers of gangsta rap.

However, Knight had a reputation as a thug. He was said to have connections to a street gang. At the time he and Dr. Dre were trying to launch their label, Knight was facing charges of attempted murder, auto theft, and carrying a concealed weapon. Dre, too, had legal issues. He was arrested for assaulting a TV host in a nightclub. Given their troubles with the law, Knight and Dre found it hard to get start-up money for their company.

"Nobody wanted to be in business with Death Row, because, unfortunately, they [other music industry executives] felt there was an element there that could be dangerous," Jimmy Iovine told an

G-FUNK

In the early 1990s, rap music was growing more popular. It was also developing new styles. Dr. Dre helped start a new style of rap called G-funk (for "gangsta funk"). It was extremely popular among rappers on the West Coast.

G-funk had a slower tempo than other rap. It used synthesizers, instruments that produce music electronically. G-funk also featured a lot of bass and keyboards. Rap songs often would **sample** other songs, meaning they would pick up parts of those songs, such as riffs, beats, and bass lines. Dre sampled heavily from George Clinton, a pioneer of funk music during the

1970s, and from Clinton's bands Parliament and Funkadelic. But instead of simply using recordings of the samples—as other rap producers typically did—Dre often used live musicians to put a new spin of the samples.

A rapper named Cold 187um, of the group Above the Law, has claimed that he is the true originator of G-funk. Dre produced Above the Law's first album for Ruthless Records. Whatever the truth of Cold 187um's claims, Dre is usually credited as the father of G-funk. *The Chronic*, his debut solo album, brought the style to a wide audience.

interviewer. "But I knew they had great music and that they were a bunch of guys who wanted to make it out of the ghetto. That's something I can understand."

Interscope gave the new company $10 million, and Death Row was started. Knight was confident the new company would succeed. He said he would make it into the "Motown of the '90s."

TAKING A CHANCE

In December 1992, Death Row Records released its first album. Called *The Chronic*, it was Dr. Dre's **debut** solo album. It also featured a young rapper Dr. Dre had discovered and signed to Death Row. His name was Snoop Doggy Dogg.

The Chronic was controversial. Most of the tracks talked about drugs and violence. There were a lot of swear words. Although Death Row was able to make the record, it didn't have the money to distribute it widely. And no major label wanted to distribute it, either. Everyone knew the record would offend a lot of people.

That's when Interscope stepped in, agreeing to distribute *The Chronic*. It might be a risky move, but Iovine and Field weren't afraid to take chances. And they had a hunch the album could sell very well. In a 2001 interview with the PBS television program "Frontline," Iovine noted:

> For the time during the late 1980s and early 1990s, outside of one or two rock bands, hip-hop was the most potent message and the most true message that was being delivered in this country. . . . Hip hop was music of the kids. They demanded it, believe me. The industry did not want it to happen. The industry did not state, "Let's get into the hip hop business or the rap business." That was absolutely not the case. The kids drove that movement.

In the mid-1990s, Snoop Dogg appeared on two of the most influential hip-hop albums: The Chronic *and his solo effort* Doggystyle. *The success of these albums made the partnership between Interscope and Death Row Records extremely profitable for both companies.*

Iovine and Field's instincts paid off. *The Chronic* eventually sold almost 4 million copies. That made it one of the best-selling albums of the decade. Dr. Dre won a Grammy Award for Best Rap Solo Performance for one of the songs, "Let Me Ride." The album showed that Interscope could be a big player in the industry. A year later, in 1993, Death Row released Snoop Doggy Dogg's album, *Doggystyle*. Dr. Dre produced this record, too. It was even more successful than *The Chronic*. It went four times platinum. Between his own music and his work with other artists, Dr. Dre was making a name for himself as one of the best producers of rap music.

TUPAC SHAKUR

Throughout the early 1990s, Interscope continued to sign more rap artists. One of them was Tupac Shakur. Shakur was a talented artist and a strong personality. He would end up influencing the direction of the label.

Rapper Tupac Shakur (left) and Death Row Records chairman Marion "Suge" Knight (right), attend a 1996 event in Los Angeles. Interscope agreed to distribute Death Row's releases despite Knight's reputation as a violent thug.

Shakur was born in Harlem, New York, in 1971. He showed an early interest in all aspects of the arts. He was interested in music, dancing, and acting. In the early 1990s, he developed his rapping skills with the groups Digital Underground and Thug Life.

Shakur was signed to Interscope after Ted Field heard a tape of the rapper. Field got his teenage daughter to listen to it. When she liked it too, Field was convinced that Shakur should get a record deal.

In 1991, Interscope released Shakur's album *2Pacalypse Now.* It went gold. Shakur's second album, released in 1993, went platinum. That success was topped by 1995's *Me Against the World.* The album rocketed to the top of the Billboard 200 charts. It sold more than 2 million copies. Shakur was now one of rap's biggest stars.

Like other rap artists, however, he'd had many run-ins with the law. In early 1995, he began serving a prison sentence for assaulting a young female fan. But Shakur's lawyers believed he hadn't received a fair trial. They appealed his conviction. A judge ruled that there were valid grounds for the appeal. The judge permitted Shakur to go free while the case was being decided. But the rapper didn't have enough money to post bail. Suge Knight, the head of Death Row, wanted Shakur on his label. So the two struck a deal: Knight would post Shakur's $1.4 million bail, and Shakur would join Death Row.

In February 1996, Death Row released Shakur's *All Eyez on Me,* which included the hits "How Do U Want it" and "California Love." This double-album sold 9 million copies.

All Eyez on Me was just one in a string of hit albums released by Death Row Records. The label had become a major force in the rap music industry. But it was headed for trouble. And because of their close relationship, Interscope would be pulled into the controversy.

facing the music

Rap music was making money for Interscope. However, rap artists, as well as other people who worked in the business, often got into trouble. Many of them were from rough neighborhoods. Many of them came from broken families. They were used to violence and fighting. Sometimes they brought this street behavior inside the doors of their record labels. In addition, gangsta rap was getting more and more of a "bad rap" from the public. Rap music was facing a lot of pressure from without and within.

OPPONENTS

Tupac Shakur's 1991 album, *2Pacalypse Now*, had caused a lot of controversy. On tracks such as "Trapped," "Souljaz Story," and "Violent,"

Shakur had negative things to say about the police. In 1992, a Texas policeman was killed by a teenager who had been listening to the album. Many people claimed that the teen had been influenced by *2Pacalypse Now*. Vice President Dan Quayle said, "There is absolutely no reason for a record like this to be published by a responsible corporation. Today I am suggesting that the Time Warner subsidiary Interscope Records withdraw this record. It has no place in our society." However, Interscope refused to pull back the album.

A few years later, in 1995, Death Row Records was preparing to release the debut album of the rap duo Tha Dogg Pound. The album,

BEST NEW MUSIC

Rap music began informally. It started in basements and on city streets. At first, the music industry took little notice. But as rap grew up, the music industry recognized it as a separate genre, or type, of music. The industry also began to see rap's potential for commercial success.

One major sign that rap had arrived occurred in 1987. That year, the Recording Industry Association of America (RIAA) gave rap its own category. The RIAA—an organization for recording artists and companies—uses categories to group different types of music and keep track of sales.

Another signal that rap was around to stay came in 1989, when the Grammy Awards added the category "Best Rap Performance." Given by the National Academy of Recording Arts and Sciences, the Grammys recognize outstanding achievements in the music industry. In 1991, the rap Grammy was divided into two different awards. One was for the best solo performance, and the other for the best group performance. In 1996, the Grammys added another award, for Best Rap Album.

called *Dogg Food*, contained graphic descriptions of acts of violence. The lyrics, in the view of many people, were also **obscene**. It wasn't the first time Interscope would be distributing a controversial album. This time, however, the company faced a lot of **publicity** before the album even came out.

C. Delores Tucker, a well-known figure in the African-American community, bought a small amount of stock in Time Warner. This meant that Tucker owned a tiny piece of the company that owned Interscope. Owning Time Warner stock gave Tucker the right to speak at the company's annual shareholders' meeting. Tucker said Time Warner should not have anything to do with albums such as *Dogg Food* because gangsta rap contained messages that were harmful to youths. She said she had decided to take on the "gangsters in the suites rather than the gangsters in the streets." By this, she meant that she would fight the record companies who distributed this kind of music.

Tucker insisted that she didn't dislike rap music in general. She said that gangsta rap could have gone a different direction,

In the early 1990s, political leaders like Vice President Dan Quayle (top) and Senator Bob Dole (bottom) were critical of gangsta rap.

with rappers writing "songs full of hope and faith." However, she added, "They weren't paid to sing that."

Tucker's protests attracted a lot of national attention. Bob Dole, a *conservative* U.S. senator who was running for president, agreed with the civil rights activist.

Around this time, Congress was considering new laws regarding the cable television industry. Time Warner was a huge corporation, and cable was a big part of its business. By comparison, rap music—

Civil Rights activist C. Delores Tucker led a national campaign against the violence-filled lyrics of most gangsta rap songs.

while highly profitable—was much less important. Time Warner executives didn't want the negative publicity surrounding gangsta rap to hurt its interests in cable TV. However, the company couldn't control what Interscope did. If Field and Iovine wanted to distribute *Dogg Food*, Time Warner was powerless to stop them.

Dogg Food was, in fact, released in October 1995 with Interscope's support. Iovine later told the *New York Times,* "Our charter was to make deals with people that we really respect and give them complete and absolute control over their lives. We felt that if we did that, we would [succeed]."

In the wake of the controversy, Time Warner executives decided to cut their ties with Interscope. Time Warner sold its stock in the company back to Interscope for $100 million. That's a lot of money, but it was much less than the stock was actually worth. Only four months later, Field and Iovine sold the stock to the record company MCA. Their price was $200 million. They had doubled their money. The deal paid off for MCA, too. It had been struggling. Now it started selling more records.

> **FAST FACT**
>
> MCA was mostly owned by another company called Seagram. Seagram's chief executive officer (CEO), Edgar Bronfman Jr., wrote songs for Celine Dion and Dionne Warwick.

TURF WARS

Many rappers grew up in tough neighborhoods. Some had been involved in street gangs and were used to settling conflicts violently. Even after they had achieved success in the music industry, some rappers continued to be associated with violence.

It was common for rappers to brag about their toughness in their songs. Insulting other rappers was also an accepted part of the rap music world. But many people believe that Death Row executive Suge Knight raised the stakes at the Source Hip-Hop Music Awards in August 1995. Knight, onstage to present an award, used the occasion to insult and challenge Sean "Puffy" Combs. Combs was head of Bad Boy Entertainment, a rap label based in New York City. The incident helped spark a feud between Bad Boy and Los Angeles–based Death Row Records. Soon a rivalry between East Coast and West Coast rappers had emerged.

The feud was waged on rap albums, as members of the rival camps exchanged insults and threats. But actual incidents of violence broke out on several occasions.

Tupac Shakur put himself in the middle of the East Coast–West Coast feud. He had been an East Coast rapper. But after signing with Death Row, he viciously insulted Sean Combs and one of Bad Boy Entertainment's top artists, Biggie Smalls, also known as the Notorious B.I.G. The rapper, whose real name was Christopher Wallace, had been Shakur's friend. But Shakur believed Wallace and Sean Combs had tried to kill him. In at least one of his songs, Shakur vowed revenge.

Meanwhile, Death Row Records was having problems. Cofounder Suge Knight was in trouble with the law again. Violence surrounded the label. Rumors of gang activity swirled. The federal government began investigating charges that Death Row was doing business illegally.

In June 1996, Dr. Dre left Death Row Records. He was

> **FAST FACT**
>
> In 1996, Dr. Dre released *Dr. Dre Presents the Aftermath*. The album included a song called "Been There, Done That." It was his way of saying he was finished with gangsta rap.

tired of all the controversy the label stirred up. Dre formed his own record label, called Aftermath Entertainment. Its records were also distributed by Interscope.

A few months after Dre's departure, Death Row would lose another of its big stars. On the night of September 7, 1996, Tupac Shakur

Bad Boy Entertainment founder Sean "Puffy" Combs (center) poses with members of his group Diddy-Dirty Money (Dawn Richard, left, and Kalenna Harper). Interscope distributes Diddy-Dirty Money's 2010 album Last Train to Paris.

FAST FACT

After Tupac Shakur's death, Interscope continued to sell his music. In his song "Child Support," rapper Ice Cube criticized Interscope for this decision.

was the victim of a drive-by shooting in Las Vegas, Nevada. He died six days later.

No one was ever charged with Shakur's murder. But many people assumed it was part of the East Coast–West Coast rap feud. Six months later, in what was widely believed to be a revenge slaying, Shakur's rival Biggie Smalls was himself murdered in a drive-by shooting in Los Angeles.

By this time, Suge Knight was behind bars. He had participated in a beating on the night Tupac Shakur was murdered. That led to a nine-year prison sentence. With Dr. Dre gone and Knight in prison, Death Row Records began to fall apart. In January 1998, Interscope decided to stop distributing the label's records.

Making it in the Mainstream

Hard-core rap was Interscope's signature. The company made a lot of money from its releases in this *genre*. But hard-core rap wasn't the only type of music Interscope produced.

Throughout the 1990s, Jimmy Iovine and others at the company searched for new artists from a variety of genres. Interscope was rather selective, offering contracts to a relatively small number of artists. But those the company did sign tended to do quite well for Interscope. Among them were Primus, No Doubt, Nine Inch Nails, and Marilyn Manson. As a 1997 article in *Newsweek* noted, "In a business where finding a successful act is about as easy as spotting a necktie at the Grammy Awards, Interscope has assembled an unmatched array of alternative-rock and urban-music hit makers."

BRANCHING OUT

In 1991, Iovine listened to a tape from a California band called No Doubt. The group had been working for several years but had not achieved any real success. Iovine liked their sound, however. And he liked the group's young lead singer, Gwen Stefani. The group's first two albums for Interscope sold poorly. But Iovine continued working with No Doubt. He helped the band develop a stronger sound and image. He also put Stefani squarely at the front. The result? No Doubt scored a huge hit with its third album, *Tragic Kingdom*, which was released in 1995. The album sold 8 million copies.

Usually, it's the artist who hopes a record company will offer a contract. But occasionally, a record company is desperate to bring an artist on board. Such was the case with Nine Inch Nails, an industrial rock act from Cleveland, Ohio. Iovine loved Nine Inch Nails and its leader, Trent Reznor. And he was willing to push the envelope to bring the group to Interscope. While Reznor wasn't happy with his current company, TVT Records, TVT wasn't willing to let Nine Inch Nails go. Iovine, however, was persistent. He called Steve Gottlieb, the head of TVT. Then he called

Interscope not only released successful albums by No Doubt, the label has also produced and distributed solo work by the band's lead singer, Gwen Stefani.

Interscope released the second album by Nine Inch Nails, The Downward Spiral, *in 1994. Trent Reznor (pictured) remained with the label until 2008.*

again, and again, and again— every day for a year.

Eventually, Gottlieb gave in. In 1992, he agreed to allow Nine Inch Nails to sign with Interscope. Iovine agreed to allow Reznor to create his own label, Nothing Records, which would be a joint venture of Interscope and TVT. Interscope would distribute the releases of Nothing Records.

Nothing Records lasted a dozen years, folding in 2004. It didn't sign many acts or make a lot of money. However, it did bring in one notable act. Marilyn Manson was a "shock rock" group known for its outrageous behavior and music.

Interscope was growing, and the music industry took note. Russell Simmons was the head of a competing label, the hip-hop powerhouse Def Jam Music Group. "Jimmy [Iovine] has become a real thorn in my side in the [black music] business," Simmons observed in 1997. "He's got the alternative rock world, the alternative black world, and he's just starting. It's pretty scary."

Interscope would become even more powerful in the late 1990s. In 1998, MCA acquired Polygram, another huge music company. Polygram included Geffen Records and A&M Records. Polygram combined Geffen and A&M with Interscope. The result was a superpower label called Interscope/Geffen/A&M (IGA). The next year, MCA was renamed Universal, the name it still has. IGA was the most important label within Universal.

EMINEM

Iovine was open to new artists. He didn't care where they came from or who found them. An *intern* at Interscope heard a rapper named Eminem on the radio. He was impressed. He got a copy of the tape and gave it to Iovine. As soon as Iovine heard it, he phoned rap producer Dr. Dre, who was now working with Interscope. Two days later, Dre and Eminem were in a recording studio.

Eminem's debut album, *The Slim Shady LP*, came out in 1999. "Slim Shady" was a character that Eminem created. The character was extremely violent. Eminem was widely condemned for songs that, his critics charged, encouraged violence and expressed contempt for women. But *The Slim Shady LP* was popular with fans. It sold more than 4 million copies.

Eminem's next album, released in 2000, was called *The Marshall Mathers LP*. Marshall Mathers is the rapper's real name. Within a week of its

> **FAST FACT**
>
> Back when records were pressed on vinyl, "LP" referred to an album. The letters stood for "long playing." The two-sided LP, which usually measured 12 inches in diameter, could contain up to 45 minutes of music in all. LPs were played at a speed of 33 1/3 revolutions per minute (rpm). Singles were released, one per side, on 7-inch vinyl records. These records were played at 45 rpm. Hence they were commonly referred to as "45s."

Eminem attends a premiere of his 2002 movie 8 Mile. *The rapper has maintained a relationship with Interscope that has brought new performers to the label.*

release, *The Marshall Mathers LP* had sold nearly 1.8 million copies. This made it the fastest-selling rap album in history, according to the music magazine *Rolling Stone.* Eventually, more than 10 million copies of the album would be sold in the United States.

Eminem followed up with a third album, called *The Eminem Show.* Released in 2002, it was another smash hit. *The Eminem Show* soared to number one on the Billboard 200 charts. It went eight times platinum.

Rolling Stone ranked Eminem at number 82 on its 100 Greatest Artists of All Time list. *Vibe,* another music magazine, named him the "Best Rapper Ever." Eminem has won the Grammy Award for Best Rap Album a record-setting four times: for *The Slim Shady LP, The Marshall Mathers LP, The Eminem Show,* and 2009's *Relapse.*

The rapper has also starred in a popular movie, *8 Mile.* The 2002 film told the story of an up-and-coming rapper from Detroit, Michigan. Although the movie isn't exactly about Eminem's life, a lot of it is similar to his youth and early career.

In his book, *The Way I Am,* Eminem wrote, "Rap forced me to deal with people socially. . . . Hip-hop was a community where I could fit

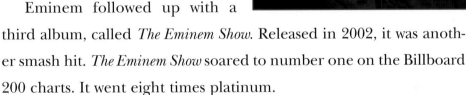

Eminem and Dr. Dre discovered rapper Curtis "50 Cent" Jackson, and collaborated with Interscope to release his first album. Get Rich or Die Tryin' *was a major hit. Interscope eventually helped 50 Cent to establish his own label, G-Unit, and distributed music by its artists.*

in, and it really didn't matter that I was white. Hip-hop made me feel like I was on a team. I felt like I was not only representing people who had my back, but also connecting them to each other. That's what hip-hop is all about for me. Always has been."

50 CENT

Eminem's success gave him influence in the music industry. He helped other artists on their way up. He heard an album by a rapper named Curtis Jackson, now known as 50 Cent. Eminem signed him to a record deal and hooked him up with Dr. Dre.

Many rap songs tell of the hard lives of inner-city African Americans. 50 Cent lived that life. His mother was murdered when he was 12. He made money selling drugs and got arrested. The bright spot in his life was rapping. He met Run-DMC's Jam Master Jay, who taught him how to improve his rapping skills.

"Because of rappers like the Notorious B.I.G., Tupac and Snoop Dogg—all had sold millions of records talking about the streets—I didn't feel like I had to compromise who I was to make music," 50 Cent wrote in his book, *From Pieces to Weight*. "I wrote about the things I had seen in my life and what was going on in the 'hood."

In 2003, 50 Cent's debut album, *Get Rich or Die Tryin'*, came out. It took the top spot on the Billboard 200 chart and eventually sold about 8 million copies. His next album, 2005's *The Massacre*, sold about 5 million copies. Neither of his other two albums for Interscope, *Curtis* (2007) or *Before I Self Destruct* (2009), sold nearly as well. In 2010, 50 Cent left the label.

GOD'S PROPERTY

In 1997, Interscope released an album called *God's Property* from a Christian gospel performer, Kirk Franklin (pictured). Coming from a label that had made its name with controversial, hard-core rap acts, the move might have surprised many people. It shouldn't have. Interscope cofounder Jimmy Iovine wasn't trying to stir up trouble with the label's hard-core rap releases. He was just trying to make money. And that was something he was good at, whether the music was rap or gospel.

God's Property—with its main single, "Stomp"—went platinum in three months. Eventually it sold more than 3 million copies. That made it the best-selling gospel album of all time. It also topped the Billboard gospel and R&B/hip hop charts, and it won several Grammy Awards.

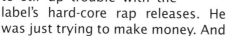

The Black Eyed Peas—apl.de.ap, Fergie, Taboo, and will.i.am—are among Interscope's most successful acts.

BLACK EYED PEAS

Interscope hit it big with another hip-hop group, the Black Eyed Peas. The Peas weren't a straight rap group. Instead, they combined hip-hop with a pop sound and attitude. They used a strong female vocalist, and they played with a live band.

In 1998, the Black Eyed Peas released their debut album, *Behind the Front*. Since then, the group has achieved phenomenal success. In 2009, their album *The E.N.D.* produced two quick hits. The singles "I Gotta Feeling" and "Boom Boom Pow" went to numbers one and two on the Billboard Hot 100 chart—at the same time! That was a *milestone* only a handful of artists have ever achieved. Also, with "Boom Boom Pow," the Black Eyed Peas had produced more Top 40 hits than any other group for the whole decade.

TAKING CHANCES

Interscope had a solid lineup of artists. Its groups covered all genres of music, from alternative rock to pop to hip-hop. The company had a reputation for taking chances. "I don't care if it's eight donkeys in a row playing harmonicas," Iovine told *Time.* "If they all look great and sound great, I'll sign 'em."

In part because of his good instincts, the risks Interscope took often paid off. But in music, people's tastes are always changing. And soon, the business itself would start changing.

5

a changing business

B y 2000, the music industry—like the rest of society—was entering the digital age. Major changes in the way record companies did business were on the way. The industry would have to adapt.

In the past, music lovers had been introduced to new music largely by listening to the radio. When they liked what they heard on the air, many people would take the next step: they would go to a record store and buy the album. By the turn of the new millennium, however, this model was beginning to become outdated. Music fans no longer needed radio disc jockeys to introduce them to new music. They could find that music on the Internet. And they no longer had to go to a record store to obtain a new CD for their collection. They could download the music without ever having to leave home. Most alarming for the music industry, through file-sharing programs people could download music without paying for it.

FARM CLUB

Jimmy Iovine already knew how to tap into talent. Now he wanted to tap into technology as well. Iovine and his boss, Doug Morris—the head of Universal Music Group—began talking about how they could use the Web to promote music. The result was a project called "Farm Club." The name of this Internet-based record company, which was launched in 2000, came from the term for a minor-league baseball team associated with a major-league team. At the farm club, players hone their skills. If they perform well enough, they may get the call to play on the major-league team.

Interscope uses its Website, www.interscope.com, to promote its artists. It provides links to videos, news, and information about upcoming tours and album releases.

In a similar fashion, the musical Farm Club would function as a proving ground for new artists. If they did well enough, they could get signed to a record contract. First, hopeful musicians uploaded their songs to a Web site. Then, people gave feedback. Anyone with a computer connection could log on, listen, vote, and comment. A&R executives at Interscope/Geffen/A&M would have a chance to spot new talent. But ordinary fans would also get to hear, and weigh in on, new music. After the initial stage, certain artists were chosen to be on a TV show.

Farm Club didn't follow the usual steps involved in most recording contracts. But Iovine didn't want business executives making all

INTERSCOPE DIGITAL DISTRIBUTION

With the Internet, more artists like the idea of "DIY" (do it yourself) distribution. Why wait around trying to get a record deal when anyone can put up music on the Internet in just a few minutes?

In late 2009, Interscope started its own digital distribution system. Through Interscope's company Web site, artists can sign up for a free account. They upload their songs and artwork onto the site. Then, people can buy the music through online music stores like iTunes or Amazon. Interscope pays the profits back to the artist.

In addition, A&R executives at the company listen to what's being put up. If they like it, they might offer the artist a contract.

"THE NEXT"

Who's next? That was the premise of a television miniseries called *Interscope Presents "The Next Episode."* The miniseries, inspired by Eminem's movie *8 Mile*, aired in 2003 on the cable network Showtime.

Over six episodes, the show told the stories of several rappers as they worked to break through and become successful artists. The show picked contestants from cities across the United States. It detailed their everyday lives, their hopes, and the struggles they faced in trying to make it as a rap artist. The contestants then competed against one another in rap battles to be chosen as the winner.

the decisions. Instead, he thought that musicians had a much better sense of what kind of music fans wanted. And Farm Club's fan participation could allow musicians to build a large following even before a record contract had been signed.

iTUNES

Although Farm Club was an interesting idea, it didn't catch on. By 2001 it was finished. However, Iovine still believed that technology was the key to the music industry's future.

If people could download as much music as they wanted, for free, it would hurt record companies. But what if customers could get the music easily online, though they still had to pay for it? That might help the labels.

=== FAST FACT ===

In 2001, Interscope cofounder Ted Field left the label. He formed another record label, called ARTISTdirect Records. It closed down in 2003.

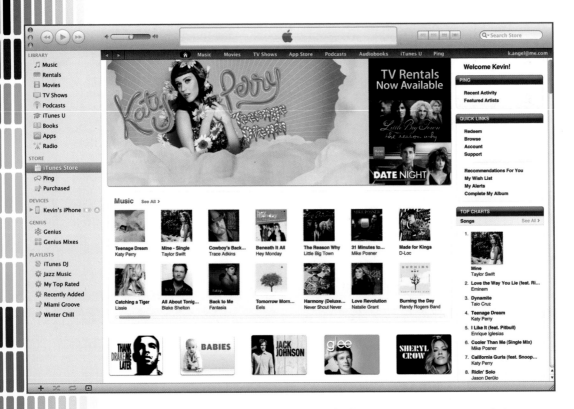

The Universal Music Group labels, including Interscope, participate in the Apple iTunes Music Store as a way to sell digital downloads of their music.

Apple Computer came up with a solution. Its idea was to create a portable music player—the iPod. Customers could get songs for their iPods from an online store called iTunes. Iovine met with the head of Apple, Steve Jobs. He was impressed with what Jobs was trying to do. Dr. Dre was another fan. At first, Dre didn't want to give up the digital rights to his songs. However, he agreed to go to Apple's offices and play around with the service for a while. Afterward, Dre changed his tune. He had seen other efforts to make songs available to customers digitally, but believed Apple had the best system. He remarked, "Man, somebody finally got it right."

In the years to come, Iovine and other music executives became unhappy with iTunes. They believed that the way the company priced and distributed music was unfair. However, their early support helped iTunes succeed.

LADY GAGA

Today, the ability to get music online has helped many artists. Look at Interscope artist Lady Gaga. She's extremely popular on the Internet. On various Web sites, her songs have gotten hundreds of millions of "hits"—the number of times people click to listen. She also sells a lot of music online, mostly through iTunes.

Only a few years ago, Lady Gaga was a struggling performer and songwriter in New York. She briefly had a deal with Def Jam records, but it didn't go anywhere. Then, in 2008, an Interscope producer named Vincent Herbert saw a video of her. He hired her to write songs.

Iovine and others at Interscope quickly recognized her talent as a performer. Interscope released her debut album, *The Fame*, in 2008. It reached number two on the Billboard 200 charts.

Interscope has a special kind of business arrangement with Lady Gaga called a "360 deal." A circle has 360 degrees, and the name refers to a "full-circle" relationship. In a 360 deal, the

> **FAST FACT**
> Lady Gaga's real name is Stefani Joanne Angelina Germanotta.

record label provides an act with enough money to market and promote itself. The label pays for advertising and for the cost of concert tours. In return, the artists pay back to the label part of all the money

Lady Gaga has had many hit singles and won five Grammy Awards. Since 2008, she has been one of Interscope's most successful and profitable artists.

they make. This includes money from record sales, as well as income from live performances, merchandise sales, or *endorsements* such as commercials.

Artists often inspire new styles or trends, but Lady Gaga takes it to an extreme. Her fashion sense, and her eye-catching hair and make-up, have gotten her endorsement deals from an array of companies. Under the 360 deal, Interscope makes money from all her endorsement deals as well as her music sales.

* * * * *

The music industry has changed a lot in the last two decades. How people listen to and buy music may change more in the future. But however it shakes out, one thing won't change: people will still want to hear good music. That's what guided Interscope back when it started, and that's what keeps the label running.

Interscope is always on the lookout for talented artists. In 2011, the label signed American Idol *performer* Pia Toscano, and released her first album in the fall of that year.

new directions

As his company turned 20 years old, Jimmy Iovine continued to see his main job as discovering artists. That's the job of everyone else at Interscope, too. When friends, company interns, and other artists hear something interesting, they bring it to Iovine to get his take on it. "It can come from anywhere," Iovine said in a 2007 interview.

> *This company is very agile and very light on its feet. . . . It's not hard to get a record deal here. It's just that the heat has to come with it. It's got to be really, really good. . . . Personally I look for . . . something original, something different, something that is where the songs are there, but the spirit is also there.*

Iovine still remembers his early days working with great artists. "I've always wanted to bring to this record company the intensity and drive of those artists," he told the *Los Angeles Times*. "Every artist can't be Springsteen or Lennon or you'd only have two artists on your label, but you want to encourage everyone to reach for that spark of passion that I saw every day in them."

RELATIONSHIP WITH ARTISTS

Iovine has always said that Interscope is sensitive to—and does its best to accommodate—the wishes of artists. On multiple occasions, Iovine

MARK WILLIAMS SCOPES TALENT

In 2005, Interscope topped another chart. It was not a song or album this time, but a person. In a list of the top 100 A&R executives, from the online music database and magazine *HitQuarters*, Mark Williams came in at number one.

After joining Interscope in 2001, Williams worked with such artists as Gwen Stefani, Beck, the Hives, Queens of the Stone Age, M.I.A., the Yeah Yeah Yeahs, and Marilyn Manson. Williams helped sign some of those acts. However, in an interview with *HitQuarters* he said that most of his work happens after artists are already with the label and ready to record.

Each act has strengths and weaknesses. Williams's job is to help identify what those are, then figure out how to work with them. For example, when he worked with Gwen Stefani on her solo debut album, Williams knew she needed to write some songs. He helped match her up with other musicians who would be a good fit. The result was *Love. Angel. Music. Baby.* The album was released in late 2004. By the end of 2005, it had gone quadruple-platinum.

"There is so much glitter these days that competes for people's attention. Not just music, but every form of entertainment," Williams told an interviewer. "The artists who ultimately win are the ones who are doing something really special. I don't think you can calculate something to be truly different. It has to be true to itself."

Trent Reznor brought the "shock rock" group Marilyn Manson to Interscope in 1994. The group released seven successful albums on Interscope before leaving the label after 2009's The High End of Low.

has given complete creative control to his artists by helping them set up their own record labels. For example, after Dr. Dre left Death Row Records, he started his own label, called Aftermath Entertainment, which was part of Interscope. In 1999, Eminem had proved his ability to sell records, so Shady Records was set up under Interscope. In 2003, 50 Cent got a label called G-Unit Records. Another Interscope band, Nine Inch Nails, created Nothing Records, which signed Marilyn Manson. The will.i.am music group was set up for rapper will.i.am, a member of the Black Eyed Peas. In 2010, Justin Timberlake created Tennman Records.

But sometimes these arrangements don't work out. In 2007, Nine Inch Nails released its album *Year Zero* in Australia. Frontman Trent Reznor objected to the price. He said it was way too expensive. (It was selling for about $29.) In a post on the band's Web site, Reznor said that he had asked Interscope why the company was charging so much. He said a representative for Interscope explained: "We know

Interscope has benefitted from products that are produced or endorsed by its stars, such as Dr. Dre's line of headphones or Mary J. Blige's line of sunglasses.

you have a real core audience that will pay whatever it costs when you put something out—you know, true fans." Reznor observed with disgust, "I guess as a reward for being a 'true fan' you get ripped off."

Year Zero was the last album Nine Inch Nails would do for Interscope. Later that year, the band said it had fulfilled its contract and left the label. However, instead of signing with another company, the group decided to branch out on its own. In 2008, it released an album that was made available online for fans to download.

KNOWING THE MARKET

Popular music has always been about more than just music. Hip-hop is no exception. Today, hip-hop is about a whole lifestyle. It is expressed through music, clothing, and other merchandise. It's about attitude.

Troy Marshall is a vice president of rap promotion and lifestyle marketing for Interscope. Marshall started his music career with MCA Records. He showed that he understood the urban lifestyle. He didn't just watch it. He lived it.

Marshall told an interviewer that marketing was especially important with hip-hop music. In 2010, Dr. Dre came out with a new line of high-end headphones called "Beats." To promote them, he and Jimmy Iovine gave some to the Boston Red Sox, a professional baseball team. The players wore them on TV. Interscope also used the headphones to promote Dr. Dre's new song, "Under Pressure," which he did with Jay-Z. Another deal was in the works for Mary J. Blige to launch her own line of sunglasses.

"I still believe in the music business. People are still buying records. I think people like Susan Boyle and Eminem proved that,"

Marshall said in a 2010 interview. But with free downloads getting easier, record companies have to get creative. They have to know the market. "It's all about a buzz," Marshall noted.

> If we feel a record has not got a solid buzz, or the streets are not responding to a single as we feel it should, then we will not pull the trigger on a project. We don't care who it is. It could be a well established artist or a newcomer, if the buzz is not strong enough we won't put it out.

MOVING CULTURE

At its core, Interscope is a record company. But Iovine says his vision for the company doesn't stop with music. It also includes movies, television, and anything else that might fall into the category of "popular culture."

"I'll sign anybody that's really gifted at almost anything that resembles popular culture," Iovine said in a 2007 interview with Artists House Music. "If I met a great artist, painter, sculptor, I'd back 'em. That fits right in here as far as I'm concerned. The real goal for all of us [at Interscope] is to move popular culture. That's what we're trying to do."

It seems to be working. In 2009, Interscope hit another milestone. In December, when *Billboard* released its annual list of the year's most popular songs, the top four spots were occupied by releases from Interscope artists. It was the first time in the 52-year history of the list that a single record label could claim that

FAST FACT

Billboard magazine's Hot 100 Songs of the Year list uses several factors to rank songs. They include amount of radio airplay and listeners' reactions, hard-copy sales, and digital sales.

Award-winning actress Keke Palmer signed a contract with Interscope in 2010. Her debut single was released in 2011, and the label released her first album the next year.

When singer Nicole Scherzinger (pictured) left the Interscope group Pussycat Dolls in 2010, Jimmy Iovine signed her to a recording contract. The label released Scgerzinger's first solo album, Killer Love, in 2011. Some of the songs featured other Interscope performers, such as 50 Cent and Sting.

distinction. In 2009, the Black Eyed Peas took the number one spot with "Boom Boom Pow." Next came Lady Gaga's "Poker Face" and "Just Dance," at numbers two and three. The Black Eyed Peas rounded out the top four with "I Gotta Feeling."

The Black Eyed Peas had a feeling, and so did Jimmy Iovine. When he and Ted Field started Interscope back in 1990, they dreamed big. And they dreamed differently. They saw trends. They took risks. Sometimes they made mistakes. But they always paid attention to the music people wanted to hear. By doing that, they turned a small start-up label into one of the most powerful companies in the industry. It's sold hundreds of millions of records and launched the careers of many artists. More than anything, it's met one simple goal: find good music, and get it out there.

Chronology

1970s Hip hop music is born in New York City. Jimmy Iovine begins his career in music.

1987 The Recording Industry Association of America (RIAA) adds rap music as a category.

1988 The group N.W.A. releases *Straight Outta Compton*, one of the first gangsta rap albums.

1990 Jimmy Iovine and Ted Field launch Interscope Records.

1991 Interscope releases its first albums. Death Row Records is formed. Tupac Shakur's album *2Pacalypse Now* comes out.

1992 Dr. Dre's first solo album, *The Chronic*, is released.

1995 Time Warner sells its ownership in Interscope.

1996 Interscope joins MCA. Dr. Dre leaves Death Row Records. Tupac Shakur is murdered.

1997 Suge Knight, head of Death Row Records, is sentenced to nine years in prison. The Black Eyed Peas sign with Interscope.

1998 Interscope cuts ties with Death Row Records. MCA acquires another music company, Polygram. Polygram combines Interscope with two other labels to form Interscope/Geffen/A&M (IGA). Eminem is signed to Interscope.

1999 MCA is renamed Universal Music Group. Eminem releases *The Slim Shady LP*.

Chronology

2000   Interscope launches an online record company called Farm Club.

2001   Ted Field leaves Interscope.

2004   Interscope artist Gwen Stefani releases her solo debut, *Love. Angel. Music. Baby.*

2008   Lady Gaga joins Interscope.

2009   Interscope artists Lady Gaga and the Black Eyed Peas hold the top four spots on Billboard's Hot 100 Songs of the Year list.

2010   Eminem wins his fourth Grammy award for Best Rap Album. Artists YelaWolf and Die Antwoord sign with Interscope. 50 Cent leaves Interscope.

2011   In May, Interscope releases Lady Gaga's second album, *Born this Way*. The album is a huge success, selling more than 5 million copies worldwide.

Glossary

conservative—traditional; in favor of established ways of doing things.

debut—the first appearance by a performer; to make one's first appearance.

distribute—to deliver a movie or music album to the places that show or sell the work to consumers.

endorsement—a business deal in which a famous person speaks in favor of a certain product or company in exchange for money.

genre—a category or type of artistic work.

gold—in the recording industry, official recognition that a song or album has sold 500,000 copies.

graphic—described in vivid detail.

intern—a person who works for little or no pay in order to learn about a certain business.

label—a record company.

lyrics—words to a song.

milestone—an event that marks an important accomplishment.

obscene—disgusting; morally repulsive.

one-hit wonder—term for an artist who has one very successful song, but no other hits.

Glossary

platinum—in the recording industry, official recognition that a song or album has sold a million copies.

publicity—the attention that something gets in the media.

sample—to use part of another artist's song (such as a bass line or riff) in producing a new song.

sign—to hire someone by means of a business contract.

single—a song from an album that can be bought by itself.

Further Reading

Edwards, Posy. *Lady Gaga: Me & You.* London: Orion Publishing Group, 2010.

Garofoli, Wendy. *Hip-Hop Culture.* Mankato, MN: Capstone Press, 2010.

Hamilton, Jill. *The Music Industry* (Introducing Issues with Opposing Viewpoints). Farmington Hills, MI: Greenhaven Press, 2009.

Marcovitz, Hal. *Dr. Dre.* Broomall, PA: Mason Crest Publishers, 2007.

Mattern, Joanne. *Eminem.* Broomall, PA: Mason Crest Publishers, 2007.

Sanna, E. J. *The Black Eyed Peas.* Broomall, PA: Mason Crest Publishers, 2007.

Waters, Rosa. *Hip-hop: A Short History.* Broomall, PA: Mason Crest Publishers, 2007.

Internet Resources

http://www.interscope.com/

The Web site of Interscope Records includes information on new releases and upcoming performances, as well as videos and biographical information about the label's artists.

http://www.universalmusic.com/

The Web site of Universal Music, the parent company of Interscope Records, lists information about artists and their releases. It also includes videos.

http://allhiphop.com/

This Web site is devoted to the culture of hip-hop music.

http://www.vibe.com

Vibe magazine's site offers information on all aspects of hip-hop music.

http://www.blender.com/

This Web site includes photos, videos, and reviews of new music, as well as lists that take a fun look at the music industry.

index

Entries in **bold italic** refer to captions

DIANE BAILEY has written more than a dozen nonfiction books for children and teens, on topics ranging from sports to states. Before turning to books, she worked as a journalist. She's published numerous articles for both children and adults, and covered the entertainment industry for publications such as *TV Guide* and *The Hollywood Reporter*. Now she also works as a freelance editor, helping authors who write fiction for children and young adults. Diane has two sons and two dogs. She lives in Kansas, very near a place that Dorothy once visited.